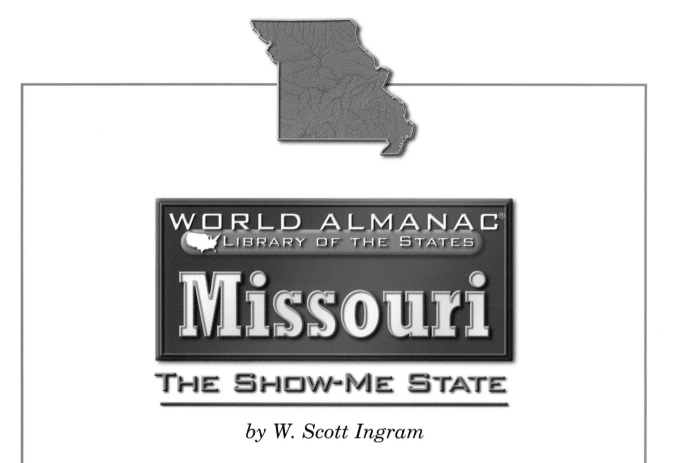

WORLD ALMANAC®
LIBRARY OF THE STATES

Missouri

THE SHOW-ME STATE

by W. Scott Ingram

Curriculum Consultant: Jean Craven,
Director of Instructional Support,
Albuquerque, NM, Public Schools

WORLD ALMANAC® LIBRARY

Please visit our web site at: www.worldalmanaclibrary.com
For a free color catalog describing World Almanac® Library's
list of high-quality books and multimedia programs, call
1-800-848-2928 (USA) or 1-800-387-3178 (Canada).
World Almanac® Library's fax: (414) 332-3567.

Library of Congress Cataloging-in-Publication Data

Ingram, Scott (William Scott).
    Missouri, the Show Me State / by W. Scott Ingram.
       p. cm. — (World Almanac Library of the states)
    Includes bibliographical references and index.
    Summary: Describes the history, geography, people, politics and government,
economy, state events and attractions, and social life and customs of Missouri,
the state that leads the nation in lead production.
    ISBN 0-8368-5139-0 (lib. bdg.)
    ISBN 0-8368-5309-1 (softcover)
    1. Missouri—Juvenile literature. [1. Missouri.] I. Title. II. Series.
F466.3.I54 2002
977.8—dc21   2002016890

This edition first published in 2002 by
World Almanac® Library
330 West Olive Street, Suite 100
Milwaukee, WI 53212 USA

This edition © 2002 by World Almanac® Library.

Design and Editorial: Bill SMITH STUDIO Inc.
Editor: Kristen Behrens
Assistant Editor: Megan Elias
Art Director: Jay Jaffe
Photo Research: Sean Livingstone
World Almanac® Library Project Editor: Patricia Lantier
World Almanac® Library Editors: Jaqueline Laks Gorman, Jim Mezzanotte, Monica Rausch
World Almanac® Library Production: Scott M. Krall, Tammy Gruenewald,
  Katherine A. Goedheer

Photo credits: pp. 4-5 © PhotoDisc; p. 6 (bottom left) © Library of Congress, (top right)
© PhotoDisc, (bottom right) © Corel; p. 7 (top) © Gutenberg-Ritchter, (bottom) © PhotoDisc;
p. 9 © Bettmann/CORBIS; p. 10 (bottom) © Corel; (inset) © Library of Congress; p. 11 St. Joseph
CVB; p. 12 © Richard Cummins/CORBIS; p. 13 Dover; p. 14 courtesy of Springfield CVB; p. 15
© Eliot Elisofon/TimePix; p. 17 Kansas City CVB; p. 18 © PhotoDisc; p. 19 © Library of Congress;
p. 20 (left to right) courtesy of Springfield CVB, © PhotoDisc, © PhotoDisc; p. 21 (left to right)
© PhotoDisc, courtesy of Hannibal CVB, © CORBIS; p. 23 © PhotoDisc; p. 26 © Corel; p. 27
© William F. Campbell; p. 29 © Library of Congress; p. 30 © Gary Brady/TimePix; p. 31 © Library
of Congress; p. 32 courtesy of Kansas City CVB; p. 33 © John Biever/TimePix; p. 34 © Mike
Segar/TimePix; p. 35 © Corel; p. 36 Springfield CVB; p. 37 (top) courtesy of Lake of the Ozarks
Convention and Visitor Bureau, (bottom) courtesy of Missouri State parks; p. 38 (left) courtesy
of Hannibal CVB, (right) Dover; p. 39 © PhotoDisc; p. 40 © TimePix; p. 41 (top) © Comstock,
(bottom) © Artville; pp. 42-43 © Library of Congress; p. 44 (top) © Corel, (center) © Artville,
(bottom) © Corel; pp. 44-45 courtesy of Hannibal CVB

Printed in the United States of America

1 2 3 4 5 6 7 8 9 06 05 04 03 02

Missouri

Plenty to Show for Itself

Missouri is the "Show-Me" state, and it has plenty to show for itself. It is rich in historic interest, natural beauty, and cultural vitality. The nation's two mightiest rivers — the Mississippi and Missouri — flow through the state of Missouri and have been carrying people and goods to and through the region for hundreds, if not thousands, of years. The state was at the center of the Native American Hopewell culture. The Hopewell left their mark on the land with large earthen mounds.

As Europeans arrived in the area that would become Missouri, they used the region's many rivers to explore the terrain and trade with local Native peoples. In the early nineteenth century, U.S. explorers Meriwether Lewis and William Clark traveled up the Missouri River into the wilds of the newly acquired Louisiana Purchase territory. Later in the century, Missouri was a jumping-off point for intrepid souls moving west in search of gold or land.

Not everyone left Missouri, however, and the cities of Kansas City and St. Louis became major cultural and transportation centers. Steamboats and railroads carried goods through the state to world markets. The state has provided more than manufactured goods and farm products. It has also given the world great thinkers and leaders. In his writings and travels, Mark Twain carried the spirit of his Hannibal boyhood with him, while U.S. president Harry S. Truman managed affairs of state with the no-nonsense attitude of his native Missouri.

The pilot of the first airplane to cross the Atlantic Ocean was not from Missouri, but it was the vision of a group of Missouri businessmen that made the flight possible. The plane Charles Lindbergh flew was named the *Spirit of St. Louis* and that spirit lives on, from the entrepreneurial visions of Walt Disney and J.C. Penney to the innovative poetry of T. S. Eliot to the can-do, high-flying attitude of the state's modern sons and daughters.

▶ Map of Missouri showing the interstate highway system, as well as major cities and waterways.

▼ The famous Gateway Arch towers over an old-time steamboat on the Mississippi River.

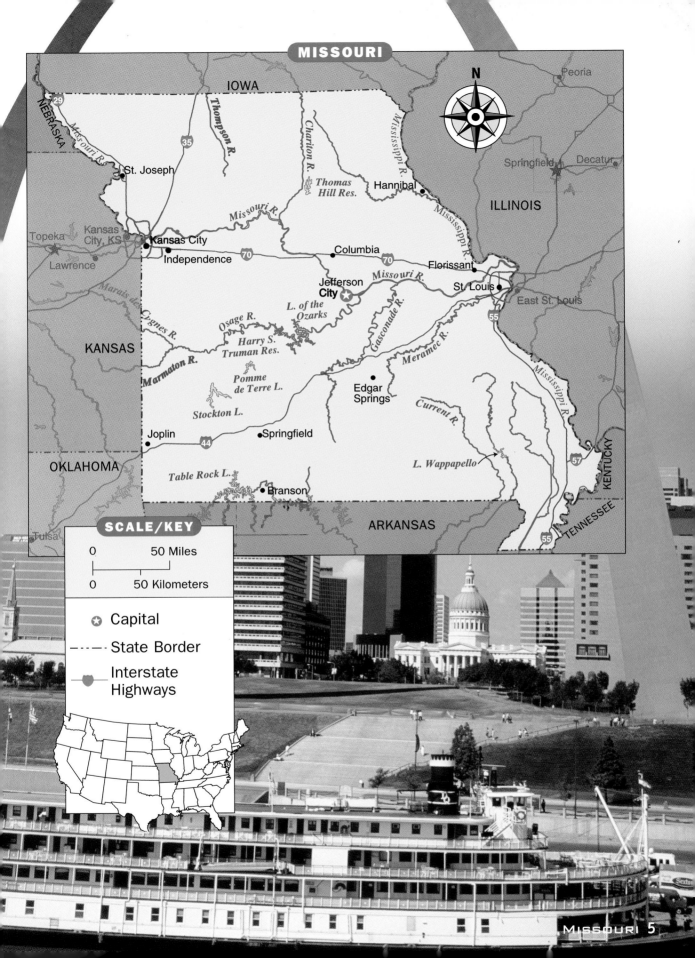

MISSOURI

IOWA

NEBRASKA

St. Joseph

Topeka

Kansas City, KS

Lawrence

KANSAS

OKLAHOMA

Tulsa

Missouri R.

Thompson R.

Charlton R.

Thomas Hill Res.

Missouri R.

Kansas City

Independence

Columbia

Jefferson City

L. of the Ozarks

Osage R.

Harry S. Truman Res.

Marais des Cygnes R.

Marmaton R.

Pomme de Terre L.

Stockton L.

Joplin

Springfield

Table Rock L.

Branson

Mississippi R.

Hannibal

Springfield

Decatur

Peoria

ILLINOIS

Florissant

St. Louis

East St. Louis

Missouri R.

Gasconade R.

Meramec R.

Edgar Springs

Current R.

L. Wappapello

Mississippi R.

KENTUCKY

TENNESSEE

ARKANSAS

SCALE/KEY

| 0 | 50 Miles |
| 0 | 50 Kilometers |

⭐ Capital

‑‑‑‑‑ State Border

Interstate Highways

Fast Facts

MISSOURI (MO), The Show-Me State

Entered Union

August 10, 1821 (24th state)

Capital	Population
Jefferson City	39,636

Total Population (2000)

5,595,211 (17th most populous state) — *Between 1990 and 2000, the state's population increased 9.3 percent.*

Largest Cities	Population
Kansas City	441,545
St. Louis	348,189
Springfield	151,580
Independence	113,288
Columbia	84,531

Land Area

68,886 square miles (178,415 square kilometers) (18th largest state)

State Motto

"Salus Populi Suprema Lex Esto" — *Latin for* "Let the Welfare of the People Be the Supreme Law."

State Song

"The Missouri Waltz," *lyrics by J. R. Shannon, melody by John V. Eppel, arranged by Frederic Knight Logan, adopted in 1949. The song became popular after Harry Truman said it was his favorite song. It is also known as "Hush-a-bye, Ma Baby."*

State Animal

Mule — *Mules helped early settlers plow Missouri farmlands and pull wagons across the state. They were still being used to transport military supplies during World War II.*

State Aquatic Animal

Paddlefish — *This primitive creature has a cartilage skeleton like a shark and can live up to thirty years.*

State Bird

Bluebird — *The bluebird, a symbol of happiness, is native to Missouri.*

State Fish

Channel catfish

State Insect

Honeybee

State Tree

Flowering dogwood

State Flower

White hawthorn blossom

State Tree Nut

Eastern black walnut

State Mineral

Galena — *This is the major source of lead ore and represents Missouri's status as the top lead-producing state in the nation.*

PLACES TO VISIT

Harry S. Truman Library & Museum, *Independence*
This museum and library contains objects and documents connected to Harry S. Truman, the thirty-third president of the United States.

The American Jazz Museum, *Kansas City*
This museum celebrates the history of jazz. Visitors learn about jazz's African roots, discover how recordings are made, and listen to music in the museum's jazz club.

Onondaga Cave State Park, *Leasburg*
The Onondaga Cave and Cathedral Cave are filled with spectacular natural rock formations.

For other places and events, see p. 44.

BIGGEST, BEST, AND MOST

- The Gateway Arch in St. Louis, completed in 1965, is the tallest human-made monument in the United States. It stands 630 feet (192 meters) tall and commemorates Missouri's history as the gateway to western settlement.

- Bert Campaneris of the Kansas City Athletics (once a Missouri baseball team), was the first person to have played all nine positions in one game.

STATE FIRSTS

- **1897** The first successful garbage incinerator was built and used in St. Louis.

- **1904** The first Olympic games to be held in the United States were held in St. Louis. The games featured fourteen events.

- **1904** Dr. Carl Ferdinand Cori and Dr. Gerty Theresa Cori, of Washington University in St. Louis, became the first U.S. husband-and-wife team to share a Nobel Prize. The Coris won the prize for Medicine.

Shaky Ground

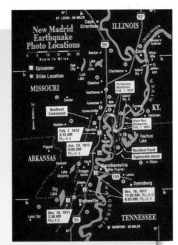

In 1811 and 1812, New Madrid was the epicenter of three earthquakes that rumbled the earth. They were among the strongest earthquakes ever to hit the United States — so strong, in fact, that they caused the Mississippi River to flow backward for a time and were felt more than 1,000 miles (1,600 kilometers) away. They may even have been more forceful than the great San Francisco earthquake of 1906. Few people lived in the affected region at the time of the earthquakes, which is the reason why there were few casualties.

Happy Trails

True to its reputation as the Gateway to the West, Missouri was the first state to have a travelers' aid society. In 1851, Bryan Mullanphy, a St. Louis man, willed about $300,000 to start a trust fund for westward emigrants. The St. Louis City Council was put in charge of distributing the money to needy pioneers.

State at the Center of a Nation

> Persons accustomed to the navigation of the Missouri and the Mississippi. . .take the precaution to load their vessels heavyest in the bow in order to avoid the danger of the concealed timber which lyes in great quantities in the beds of the rivers.
>
> — *Explorer Meriwether Lewis, May 14, 1804, at the beginning of the Lewis and Clark expedition up the Missouri River*

Long before the explorers Meriwether Lewis and William Clark set sail on their historic journey up the Missouri River in 1804, Missouri was home to various Native American cultures. About twelve thousand years ago, Native Americans settled in the Mississippi River Valley in what is today southeastern Missouri. There, they hunted and fished to feed the many people who lived in their large villages. Archaeologists have uncovered evidence that these first people also gathered plant foods, such as pigweed, goosefoot, lamb's-quarter, sunflowers, and squash.

Between approximately 800 and 400 B.C., the region and other parts of the Mississippi River Valley were home to the Hopewell culture. Archaeologists believe these people built the enormous ceremonial mounds that can still be seen in Missouri.

The First Europeans

By the time of the first major European explorations in the seventeenth century, the Hopewell people were no longer living in the region. Archaeologists believe overpopulation or war may have forced them to relocate. Another possibility is that after centuries of farming in the same fields, the soil may have become stripped of its nutrients, forcing the Hopewell to move away in search of more fertile fields. By the time Europeans arrived in the area, Native Americans were relying on hunting and gathering, rather than agriculture, to support their communities.

Two Frenchmen, Father Jacques Marquette and Louis Jolliet, were the first Europeans to explore the mouth of the Missouri River. They encountered Native Americans in what

Native Americans of Missouri
Cherokee
Delaware
Fox
Iowa
Kansa
Kaskaskia
Kickapoo
Miami
Mississippi
Missouri
Osage
Pinkashaw
Sauk
Shawnee
Wea

is now eastern and central Missouri in 1673. The Osage, who were known for being extremely tall, lived in the southern region. The Fox and Sauk lived in the north.

After Marquette and Jolliet's explorations, French trappers and fur traders began to settle in the area, trading goods along the banks of the rivers. Other settlers included French missionaries, who attempted to convert the Native Americans to Christianity. In 1682, Frenchman René-Robert Cavelier, Sieur de La Salle, explored Missouri and a vast area to the west. He claimed the territory for France, naming it Louisiana in honor of King Louis XIV. In 1735 French pioneers who traveled south down the Mississippi River from Illinois founded Missouri's first permanent white settlement. They called it Ste. Genevieve. In 1764 Pierre Laclede Liguest and René Auguste Chouteau founded St. Louis.

European Treaties

In 1763 a treaty placed all French territory west of the Mississippi River under the control of Spain. Spanish control, however, was brief. In 1800, French ruler Napoleon Bonaparte forced Spain to return the territory. Then in 1803, in order to finance military ventures in Europe, Napoleon sold the Louisiana Territory to the United States for $15 million. The next year President Thomas Jefferson

▼ A painting recreates La Salle's declaration that the territory of Louisiana belonged to France.

sent Meriwether Lewis and William Clark to investigate the new territory. They traveled approximately 8,000 miles (12,870 km), exploring the upper Missouri River, the Rocky Mountains, and the Columbia River. Along the way, they mapped their route, and when they returned to St. Louis in 1806, they reported on their travels, describing the plants, animals, and Native Americans they encountered on their journey. Their report inspired opportunity seekers, and soon, St. Louis became home to the Rocky Mountain Fur Company.

By 1812, the U.S. Congress had officially designated Missouri as a territory. Its capital, Jefferson City, was named for Thomas Jefferson, who had approved the Louisiana Purchase. With the exception of a triangle of land in the northwest that was added in 1837, the territory had the same borders then that the state has today.

By the time the Missouri Territory was formed, it had a population of more than twenty thousand people. Residents worked primarily as farmers, miners, and fur traders. During this

▼ Western encounters: A map annotated by Meriwether Lewis shows the Missouri River (*inset*). Charles Remington's painting depicts Native Americans' first sighting of Lewis and Clark (*bottom*).

time, huge numbers of settlers were arriving. They encroached on the hunting areas of the Native Americans, who responded with several violent uprisings and raids on new settlements.

After the War of 1812, more settlers arrived in the Missouri Territory. By 1820, the population had swelled to almost seventy thousand people, including more than ten thousand slaves. Many settlers were Southerners who brought slaves with them to work their lands or run their households. Life in Missouri, however, differed from life in the deep South. Although cotton was the staple crop of Southern plantations, Missouri farmers produced tobacco and raised pigs, which were sent to market on riverboats down the Mississippi River to New Orleans.

The Missouri Compromise

Five years after Missouri became a territory, its residents began taking steps toward statehood. In 1818 Congress began to debate the idea and faced a dilemma over whether slavery would be legal in the new state. When the region applied for statehood, the U.S. Senate was exactly balanced between representatives of "slave" and "free" states. Missouri's admission would disrupt this balance. Northern states did not want slavery in new territories, while Southern states did.

Prior to that time, a state was determined to be slave or free based on whether it fell above or below the Mason-Dixon Line, a line formed by the Pennsylvania–Maryland border and extending down the Ohio River to the Mississippi River. Missouri's status could not be determined that way. The Mason-Dixon Line did not extend west of the Mississippi River, and the Missouri Territory lay both north and south of the Ohio River. To solve this dilemma, the U.S. Congress devised the Missouri Compromise in 1820. Missouri was allowed to enter the Union as a slave state, while the northern state of Maine was admitted as a free state, for a total of twelve free states and twelve slave states. This maintained the balance in the Senate. Congress agreed that in the future all states north of the line formed by Missouri's southern border would be "free."

Carrying Messages West

For a brief period the city of St. Joseph was one end of the legendary mail service known as the Pony Express. Between 1860 and 1861 it ran from St. Joseph to Sacramento, California. Letters — and most important, news — were carried along the 1,966-mile (3,163-km) trail. The Express could deliver a letter in ten days or less, faster than any other service at that time.

California senator William M. Gwin and Missouri businessman William H. Russell started the service. They gathered some four hundred fast horses and designated 190 stations about 10 miles (16 km) apart. Young, lightweight men — many only in their teens — worked as riders. Each rider traveled 75 miles (121 km) or more. When he reached his destination, another rider took his place. These men earned between $100 and $150 a month — tremendous wages for that time. The Pony Express ran twenty-four hours a day, and messengers rode in good and bad weather. The Pony Express made its last run on October 26, 1861, two days after the transcontinental telegraph went into operation.

Missouri Grows

Missouri's population increased significantly from 1820 until the Civil War. St. Louis's location at the intersection of the Missouri and Mississippi Rivers made it one of the most important cities in the West. The entire state became known as the "Mother of the West" because it outfitted many of the pioneers who settled the huge region between Missouri and the Pacific Ocean. St. Louis, St. Charles, Independence, St. Joseph, and Westport Landing (today called Kansas City) were bustling starting points for westbound travelers. Some went southwest along the Santa Fe Trail from Independence. Others traveled northwest along the Oregon Trail to the Pacific Northwest, opening the way for fur trade from the West and making St. Louis the so-called "fur capital of the world" in the 1820s and 1830s.

Dred Scott and the Path to War

Despite the Missouri Compromise, the question of slavery continued to provoke bitter feelings among Americans. In 1857, a U.S. Supreme Court decision increased the tension. Dred Scott, a slave born in Missouri, was taken by his master, a U.S. army officer from Missouri, to the free state of Illinois and then to the free territory of Wisconsin. He lived on free soil for a number of years.

In 1838 Scott's master was posted back to Missouri, where he died shortly after returning. Scott then claimed he should be free because he had lived on free soil. In

The Santa Fe Trail

William Becknell originally marked the Santa Fe Trail in 1821. It served as a route for transporting goods. The trail began in Independence and ran 780 miles (1,255 km) to Santa Fe, at that time part of Mexico. Traders first used horses and pack mules to carry their goods and wares. Later, wagons were loaded with items and taken to Santa Fe, where the manufactured goods were traded for furs, horses, gold, and silver. Approximately eighty wagons used the trail each year between 1822 and 1843. When the United States acquired the New Mexico territory after the Mexican War (1846–1848), westward exploration and travel increased. In the 1850s and again in the late 1860s after the Civil War ended, as many as five thousand wagons used the trail each year. The completion of the Transcontinental Railroad in 1869 brought an end to the need for this route west.

March 1857, seven out of nine justices on the Supreme Court declared that Scott was not free and that no slave could be a U.S. citizen. The Court went on to find the Missouri Compromise unconstitutional, as it would have limited the ability of white men to own property — that is, slaves — in the free territories.

At the same time the case was being decided, many Missourians in the western area of the state feared that the newly organized and neighboring Kansas Territory would become a free state. The Kansas-Nebraska Act of 1854 had left the decision about slavery up to the residents of the territory. As a result, pro-slavery "Border Ruffians" from Missouri raced antislavery abolitionists to settle in Kansas. Scattered conflicts broke out between pro-slavery and antislavery factions in Kansas in 1856, and the state became known as "Bleeding Kansas." Kansas entered the Union as a free state in January 1861.

▲ Dred Scott drew attention to the injustice of slavery when he sued his master's widow for his freedom in 1846.

The Civil War

Missouri became the focus of national interest as the threat of war loomed. Americans in both the North and the South wondered whether Missouri would secede from the Union. In early 1861, Governor Claiborne F. Jackson, who was pro-slavery, called a state convention to make the decision. The convention voted to remain in the Union — despite the strong pro-Confederate feelings among many Missourians.

In April 1861, the first month of the war, President Abraham Lincoln called for troops from Missouri, but Governor Jackson refused to supply them. That refusal resulted in a clash between Union soldiers and the Missouri state militia, which was commanded by the governor. The Union troops defeated the militia at Boonville on June 17, 1861, and gained control of northern Missouri. Jackson and his men retreated to the southwest, where Confederate forces remained in control until March 1862, when they were defeated by Union forces. Confederate general Sterling Price's 1864 defeat in Westport marked the end of full-scale fighting in the state.

The Civil War did not put a stop to the enormous changes that were taking place in Missouri between 1850 and 1870. St. Louis, on the eastern side of the state, and Kansas City, on the western side, became important

transportation centers. After slavery ended, tenant farmers and sharecroppers, who rented small farms from large landowners, provided most of the agricultural labor in the state. This was also the era of the Wild West — the days of bank, stagecoach, and train robberies. In 1881 the governor of the state, Thomas T. Crittenden, offered a $10,000 reward for the capture — dead or alive — of a notorious bandit, Jesse James, who had been among the Missourians fighting to preserve the right to own slaves during the Civil War. The plan succeeded when Bob Ford, a member of James's own gang, shot him in the back in 1882.

Into the Twentieth Century

In 1904 the Louisiana Purchase Exposition was held in St. Louis to celebrate the centennial of the Lewis and Clark expedition. This World's Fair attracted almost twenty million visitors from the United States and other countries. One popular exhibit featured 140 automobiles that had been driven to St. Louis from cities as far away as Boston and Philadelphia. The exposition also introduced a new way to serve ice cream — in a folded waffle called a cone.

When the United States entered World War I in 1917, Missouri's mines, factories, and farms helped supply the

▲ A historical reenactment and Civil War cannon (*inset*) at the site of the Wilson Creek battle of 1861, where pro-Confederacy troops clashed with Union Army soldiers. Clashes between pro-Confederacy and Union troops were common in Missouri throughout the war.

DID YOU KNOW?

The James Gang, led by brothers Jesse and Frank James, is believed to have committed the country's first daylight bank robbery in 1866 when they stole $60,000 from the Liberty Bank.

nation's armed forces. After the war, during the 1920s and 1930s, a thriving music scene developed in Kansas City. The city became a center for a new U.S. musical form that gave its name to the age: jazz.

Like their fellow citizens throughout the nation, many Missourians lost their jobs during the Great Depression of the 1930s. The state's farmers in particular suffered because of low crop prices and drought conditions. Missouri became part of the Dust Bowl during the 1930s as wind storms swept dry soil off the plains to cause huge dust storms, destroying whatever crops remained and forcing people to leave their homes.

Many new Missouri industries, including airplane manufacturing, contributed to the Allied victory in World War II and helped pull the nation out of the Depression. In 1944 U.S. senator Harry S. Truman, a former clothes salesman from Independence, was elected vice president. He became president after President Franklin D. Roosevelt died in 1945. Truman was elected to a full term in 1948.

New electronics and aerospace industries expanded Missouri's economy during the 1950s. In the 1960s Missouri faced the legacy of its racial policies. The state constitution provided for segregated schools, but a 1954 U.S. Supreme Court decision, *Brown v. Board of Education of Topeka, Kansas,* called for desegregation. By the 1960s most public schools in Missouri were integrated.

Farm communities suffered during the mid-1980s when foreign trade restrictions were loosened and crop prices fell. Missouri also faced serious environmental issues toward the end of the twentieth century. Toxic substances, such as pesticides and fertilizer runoff — products of Missouri industry — were found in fish in the state's waterways. In the early 1980s, high levels of dioxin, a potential cancer-causing chemical, were discovered in Times Beach. The U.S. government bought and evacuated all the homes and businesses in town.

Missouri's economy remains healthy. One reason is the growth of the tourist industry. Tourism has become a billion-dollar industry, as visitors come to see what the Show-Me State has to offer.

▼ Charlie "Bird" Parker got his start as a saxophone player in Kansas City in the 1930s and became one of the most famous jazz musicians of all time. The city was then a center for jazz performance and innovation. Parker, along with jazz trumpeter Dizzy Gillespie, went on to create bebop, a unique form of jazz.

Who Makes Missouri Home?

> ...Frothy eloquence neither convinces nor satisfies me.
> I am from Missouri. You have got to show me.
> — *Congressman Willard Duncan Vandiver, speaking about Missouri in 1899. Vandiver's comment gave Missouri its official nickname, the* Show-Me State.

Since the early days of European settlement, Missouri has attracted people from around the world. First settled by a variety of Native peoples, then by French and Spanish traders, the state became home to immigrants from Europe and the eastern and southern United States in the nineteenth century. Today, Missouri's ethnic groups include people of African, German, Irish, Italian, Dutch, Scottish, and Vietnamese descent.

Missouri's population, the seventeenth largest of all the states, increased from 5,117,073 in 1990 to 5,595,211 in 2000 — an increase of 9.3 percent. That is more than double the increase of 4.1 percent from 1980 to 1990, but slightly less than the percentage of growth for the United States from 1990–2000, which was 13 percent. Fifty-five Missouri counties in the state experienced population

Age Distribution in Missouri
(2000 Census)

0–4	369,898
5–19	1,224,274
20–24	369,498
25–44	1,626,302
45–64	1,249,860
65 & over	755,379

Patterns of Immigration

The total number of people who immigrated to Missouri in 1998 was 3,588. Of that number, the largest immigrant groups were from Mexico (13.6%), India (7.5%), and Russia (7%).

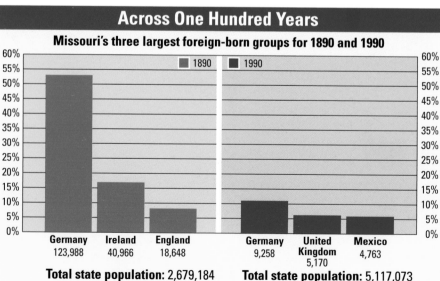

Across One Hundred Years
Missouri's three largest foreign-born groups for 1890 and 1990

1890 — Germany 123,988; Ireland 40,966; England 18,648
Total state population: 2,679,184
Total foreign-born: 234,869 (9%)

1990 — Germany 9,258; United Kingdom 5,170; Mexico 4,763
Total state population: 5,117,073
Total foreign-born: 83,633 (2%)

growth of more than 10 percent from 1990 to 2000. The fastest-growing areas of the state were those counties along a line from Columbia to Branson and around St. Louis, where the tourist industry experienced a boom. More than 50 percent of all Missourians are female, and the median age for the state population is 36.1.

The number of Missourians aged 35–54 grew almost 30 percent from 1990 to 2000. This substantial increase occurred because the baby boom generation (the large number of people born between 1946 and 1964) is aging. This is having a ripple effect on other age groups. For instance, as the baby boom generation moved into the 35–54 age group, the number of people in the 25–34 age group declined. This decline has been suggested as a reason for labor shortages in many communities.

On the older end of the demographic scale, improved health care, among other factors, now allows people to live longer. The Missouri population aged 85 and over increased by about 21 percent from 1990 to 2000.

Missouri's average population density is 81 people per square mile (31 per sq km), slightly higher than the national average of 80 people per square mile (30 per sq km). Population density varies according to region, with the

▲ There are nearly one hundred thousand farms in Missouri. More than 80 percent of these are small farms, such as those that sell produce at local farmers' markets.

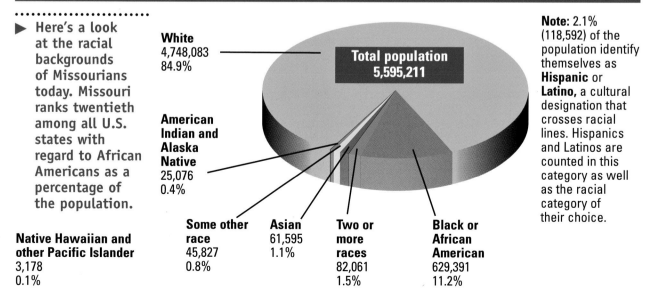

Heritage and Background, Missouri   Year 2000

► Here's a look at the racial backgrounds of Missourians today. Missouri ranks twentieth among all U.S. states with regard to African Americans as a percentage of the population.

White
4,748,083
84.9%

Total population
5,595,211

American Indian and Alaska Native
25,076
0.4%

Some other race
45,827
0.8%

Asian
61,595
1.1%

Two or more races
82,061
1.5%

Black or African American
629,391
11.2%

Native Hawaiian and other Pacific Islander
3,178
0.1%

Note: 2.1% (118,592) of the population identify themselves as Hispanic or Latino, a cultural designation that crosses racial lines. Hispanics and Latinos are counted in this category as well as the racial category of their choice.

fewest people living in the central area of the Ozark Plateau and the farming region of northern Missouri.

More than two-thirds of Missourians live in metropolitan areas. The state's major urban areas are St. Louis and Kansas City. The St. Louis metropolitan area (which includes the city of East St. Louis, Illinois) is home to 2.6 million people. Other smaller but important Missouri cities include Jefferson City, the state capital; Columbia; Joplin; and St. Joseph.

Religion

The majority of Missourians — 89 percent — identify themselves as Christians. Nearly 17 percent of people in the state are Catholic, 25 percent are Baptist, and 7 percent are Methodist. Other Christian denominations

Educational Levels of Missouri Workers (age 25 and over)	
Less than 9th grade	380,613
9th to 12th grade, no diploma	477,755
High school graduate, including equivalency	1,090,940
Some college, no degree or associate degree	756,510
Bachelor's degree	383,678
Graduate or professional degree	202,083

▼ Kansas City, which was incorporated as the City of Kansas in 1853, covers an area of more than 300 square miles (777 sq km).

in the state include Presbyterians, Episcopalians, Latter Day Saints, and Lutherans. About 1 percent of Missouri's total population is Jewish, 0.4 percent practice Native American religions, and 0.1 percent are Buddhist. There are approximately ten Islamic centers in Missouri.

Education

Education has always been important to the people of Missouri. The first school in the state was established in St. Louis in 1774 as a private elementary school. In 1818, St. Louis University became the first private university west of the Mississippi. In 1839, the University of Missouri became the first state university west of the Mississippi. It established the world's first school of journalism in 1908.

Missouri's first constitution, adopted before the state was admitted to the Union, established a public education system in 1820, but a formal school system was not in operation until 1839. The first tax-funded kindergarten in the United States opened in St. Louis in 1873. Today, all Missouri children ages seven to fifteen are required to attend school.

Missouri's first library was established in 1865 in St. Louis. For much of the nineteenth century, Missouri had a subscription library system, meaning that people in a community paid a yearly fee to read library books. Today, Missouri has approximately 350 public libraries and 70 college and university libraries. The largest library in the state is located at the University of Missouri in Columbia.

▲ Ste. Genevieve English and Classical Academy first opened in this building in 1853. The school was chartered by the territorial government in 1808 as the first school in the officially organized Missouri Territory but had not opened because it lacked funding. Ste. Genevieve Academy remained open until the Civil War disrupted classes in 1862.

A State Made by Rivers

I was never lost, but I was bewildered once for three days.
— *Daniel Boone on his travels through Missouri*

Missouri is a state of plains, rolling hills, and river valleys. The state covers 68,886 square miles (178,415 sq km) of land area. As much as 818 square miles (2,119 sq km) of the state are covered by water. More than almost any other state, Missouri's most important feature throughout its history has been its abundance of rivers. This is not surprising considering that the two largest rivers in the United States — the Mississippi and the Missouri — form north–south and east–west waterways. These huge rivers and their countless branches provide water highways for transportation. In addition, the rivers supply water for cities and industries, and dams on the rivers are used to produce hydroelectric power for homes and factories.

Rivers, Lakes, and Springs

While the Mississippi and Missouri Rivers make the state commercially and industrially important, there are many other rivers crisscrossing the state that also play important roles in the lives of Missourians. The Current River, one of Missouri's most beautiful waterways, is widely known for the game fish that abound in its fast-flowing waters. The Black, James, and St. Francis Rivers, as well as other rivers of the Ozark Plateau, are favorite spots for fishing.

Highest Point
Taum Sauk Mountain
1,772 feet (540 m) above sea level

DID YOU KNOW?
The town of Warsaw holds the state record for both the highest and lowest temperatures. Its thermometers dropped to -40°F (-40°C) on February 13, 1905. They rose to 118°F (48°C) on July 14, 1954.

▼ *From left to right:* rock formations in a Missouri cave; St. Louis as seen from the Gateway Arch; mountain mist in the Ozarks; Missouri wildlife; a riverboat near Hannibal; autumn foliage on the Missouri River.

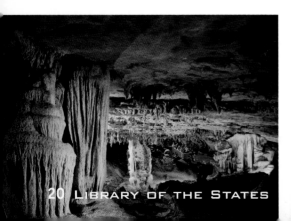

Missouri's numerous waterways and springs have allowed the people of the state to create many lakes. In fact, some of the largest artificially created lakes in the United States are found in Missouri. The largest lake in the state is the Harry S. Truman Reservoir, a body of water covering approximately 55,600 acres (22,500 hectares). Another large, artificially created lake is the Lake of the Ozarks, which covers 54,000 acres (21,852 ha). It was formed when Bagnell Dam was built on the Osage River. Table Rock, Bull Shoals, Pomme de Terre, and Taneycomo are some of the other artificially created lakes in Missouri.

Some of Missouri's rivers were created by springs — there are approximately ten thousand in the Ozark Plateau alone. The largest is Big Spring, located near Van Buren. About 286 million gallons (1,082 million liters) of water flow from it daily.

In turn, Missouri's rivers have created natural wonders. As anyone who has read Mark Twain's *The Adventures of Tom Sawyer* can tell you, caves exist in many areas of Missouri. Explorers have discovered more than 1,450 caves throughout the state. Marvel Cave, located near Branson, is one of the state's largest and includes 10 miles (16 km) of underground passages.

Lowlands, Uplands, and Plains

The state's location near the center of the United States makes it a convenient tourist destination and also contributes to its importance as an agricultural and manufacturing state. Missouri borders Iowa, Nebraska, Kansas, Oklahoma, Arkansas, Tennessee, Kentucky, and Illinois. Only Tennessee has as many border states.

The Osage Plains in western Missouri are flat prairies with low, rolling hills. This farming area is primarily devoted to growing grain crops. The Till Plains north of the Missouri

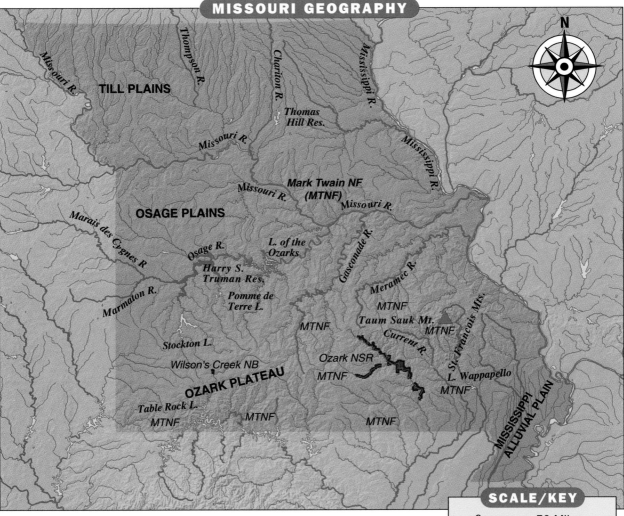

TILL PLAINS

Thompson R.

Chariton R.

Mississippi R.

Missouri R.

Thomas Hill Res.

Missouri R.

Mark Twain NF (MTNF)

Missouri R.

Mississippi R.

OSAGE PLAINS

Missouri R.

Marais des Cygnes R

Osage R.

L. of the Ozarks

Gasconade R.

Meramec R.

MTNF

Harry S. Truman Res.

Marmaton R.

Pomme de Terre L.

Taum Sauk Mt.

MTNF

St. Francois Mts.

MTNF

Stockton L.

Current R.

Ozark NSR

Wilson's Creek NB

MTNF

L. Wappapello

MTNF

OZARK PLATEAU

Table Rock L.

MTNF

MTNF

MTNF

MISSISSIPPI ALLUVIAL PLAIN

N

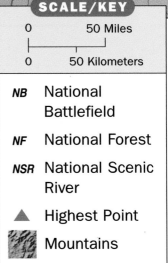

River is an area crisscrossed by streams. Millions of years ago, glaciers covered the region. These massive ice sheets ground rocks into soil and left mineral deposits behind as they retreated, creating rich soil ideal for growing corn.

The Mississippi Alluvial Plain is located in Missouri's southeastern region. While this area was once covered with mosquito-infested swamps, it has been cleared and drained. Today its rich soils are used for growing cotton, soybeans, and rice.

The Ozark Plateau, sometimes called the Ozark Mountains, in the southwestern region of the state is Missouri's largest region. The landscape features forests, hills, and small mountains, making this area a popular tourist destination. The Ozark Plateau is the largest highland area west of the Appalachians and east of the Rockies. It has many interesting natural features, including caves, springs, lakes, and streams. Missouri's waters are popular with anglers.

Missouri is also home to the St. Francois Mountains, located in the southeastern region of the state. These mountains cover approximately 70 square miles (180 sq km) and form the highest part of the state.

Climate

Missouri experiences humid, hot summers and cold winters. An average July day in Missouri reaches 78° Fahrenheit (26° Celsius). Winters in Missouri are cold, with an average temperature in January of 30°F (-1°C).

Plants and Animals

Oak and hickory trees grow in the hardwood forests that cover approximately one-third of Missouri. Other trees that grow in large numbers include ash, cottonwood, sweet gum, and shortleaf pine. Wild grape, ivy, and honeysuckle also grow in Missouri.

Missouri's native animals include white-tailed deer, red foxes, beavers, muskrats, and skunks. Birds include blackbirds, orioles, purple finches, woodpeckers, cardinals, blue jays, and mockingbirds. Missouri's streams, lakes, and rivers are home to a variety of fish, such as bass, pike, and buffalofish.

Major Rivers

Mississippi River
2,340 miles (3,765 km)

Missouri River
2,315 miles (3,725 km)

Osage River
500 miles (805 km)

▼ Red foxes eat small game, nuts, and berries. They live in every one of Missouri's 114 counties.

Making a Living in Missouri

> The traveler on the prairie is naturally
> a hunter, on the head waters of the Missouri
> and Columbia a trapper, and at the Falls of
> St. Mary a fisherman.
>
> — *Henry David Thoreau, philosopher and naturalist,*
> *in* Walden, *1854*

In the early nineteenth century, trading in furs and animal skins was the backbone of the frontier economy. Today, Missouri's economy is much more diverse — and much larger. In 2000 Missouri's exports exceeded $8.4 billion and reached more than 180 countries.

Service with a Smile, and More

Many workers, approximately 32 percent, are employed in service industries such as hospitals, law firms, and restaurants. Service industries also account for the largest part of Missouri's gross state product — the total value of all the goods and services produced in the state in a year.

About 22 percent of Missouri's employed population work in wholesale and retail trade, including wholesale trade of farm products. The wholesale grocery trade is a major area of employment. Kansas City and St. Louis, the state's two largest cities, lead retail trade in Missouri.

Real estate, finance, and insurance account for more than 6 percent of Missouri's employment. This segment is also centered in Kansas City and St. Louis. The state's largest commercial banks and insurance companies are located in St. Louis. District banks of the Federal Reserve Bank are located in both St. Louis and Kansas City.

More than 4 percent of Missouri's workers are employed in government and military positions. These include people who work in public schools and hospitals and on military bases. Transportation and shipping have long been key parts of Missouri's economy. Several railroad services run

Top Employers (of workers age sixteen and over)	
Services	31.6%
Wholesale and retail trade	21.7%
Manufacturing	18.6%
Transportation, communications, and utilities	8.1%
Finance, insurance, and real estate	6.3%
Construction	5.8%
Government and Military	4.3%
Agriculture, forestry, and fisheries	3.4%
Mining	0.2%

DID YOU KNOW?

Missouri has the third lowest cost of living in the country.

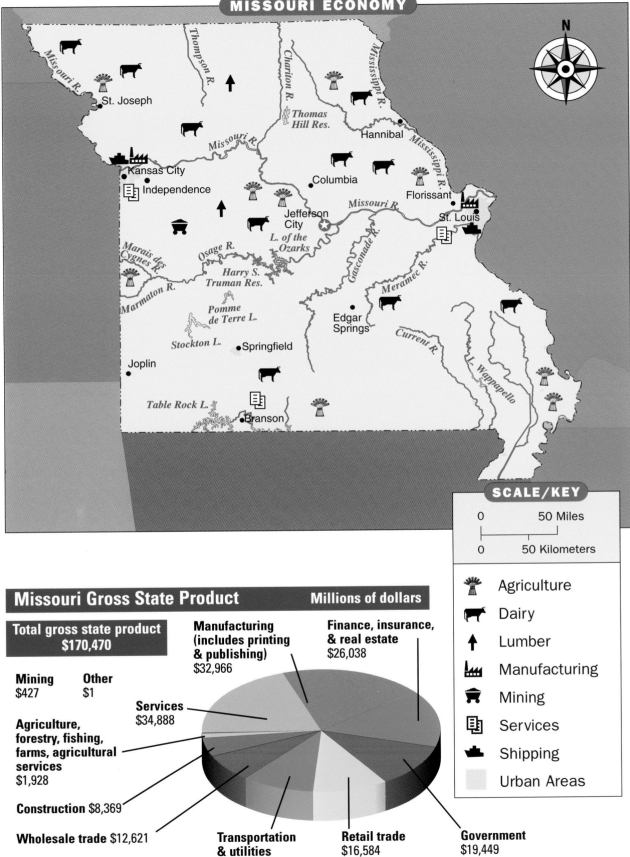

MISSOURI ECONOMY

SCALE/KEY

0 — 50 Miles

0 — 50 Kilometers

- 🌾 Agriculture
- 🐄 Dairy
- ↑ Lumber
- 🏭 Manufacturing
- 🛒 Mining
- 📑 Services
- 🚢 Shipping
- ▨ Urban Areas

Missouri Gross State Product   Millions of dollars

Total gross state product $170,470

Mining $427   **Other** $1

Manufacturing (includes printing & publishing) $32,966

Finance, insurance, & real estate $26,038

Services $34,888

Agriculture, forestry, fishing, farms, agricultural services $1,928

Construction $8,369

Wholesale trade $12,621

Transportation & utilities $17,199

Retail trade $16,584

Government $19,449

from St. Louis and Kansas City, while barges are utilized on the Missouri and Mississippi Rivers.

Manufacturing, Agriculture, and Resources

Missouri manufactures nearly $33 billion worth of goods each year. The state has more than 7,500 factories, primarily located in the Kansas City and St. Louis areas. Various types of transportation equipment — including airplanes, barges, railroad cars, truck bodies, and trailers — are the main products built in Missouri. Other manufactured items include flour, beer, and chemicals. Fertilizer, insecticides, paint, pharmaceuticals, and soap are the main chemical products. Other products made in Missouri include machinery, printed materials, and electrical equipment.

While less than 4 percent of its workforce is employed in agriculture, Missouri is still an important agricultural state. Fertile soils are a major natural resource, and farms cover approximately two-thirds of the state's land. In 2000, the state had 110,000 farms. Soybeans are Missouri's leading crop. Farms also grow corn, cotton, and wheat. Most of Missouri's soybeans are grown in the northern and southeastern parts of the state. Missouri farms also grow apples, peaches, and grapes, as well as a variety of vegetables. Animals raised for meat include hogs, beef cattle, chickens, and turkeys.

Missouri, which has extensive hardwood forests, also produces charcoal, lumber, and wood products such as oak flooring. Major mines are located in the St. Francois

▼ Soybeans, which are Missouri's most important crop, have many uses.

Mountains region. The first lead ore mines were opened there in the eighteenth century, and Missouri now leads the nation in lead production.

A Transport Center

St. Louis and Kansas City have been Missouri's transportation hubs since before the Civil War. At that time, the Mississippi River was a major north–south route for shipping and travel. In the late 1800s, the construction of railroads and highways in and out of St. Louis and Kansas City added to their importance. Today, Missouri has a total of 122,847 miles (197,661 km) of roads and highways, used by millions of Americans each year. Missouri's highway system is the sixth largest in the country. Its cities are among the nation's leading trucking centers.

Missouri has 140 public airports, two of which offer international flights. The state offers more than 1,000 navigable water miles (1,609 km), with twelve public port authorities. St. Louis is the country's second largest inland port. Boats and barges transport people and products along 490 miles (790 km) of the Mississippi River, while the Missouri has 550 miles (885 km) of usable waters.

Kansas City and St. Louis are the second and third largest railroad terminals in the United States. Missouri has 4,400 miles (7,080 km) of railroad track for transporting freight and passengers. Major rail carriers in Missouri include Burlington & Santa Fe, Union Pacific, Norfolk Southern, and Amtrak.

Tourism

Thanks to its location, Missouri is within a day's drive for 50 percent of the U.S. population. Tourism is one of the fastest growing elements of the state's economy. In 1999, travelers spent about $12.6 billion in the state, which brought in more than $574 million in tax revenue. The travel and tourism industry employs more than two hundred thousand Missourians. One of the main attractions of recent years is the historic Ozark town of Branson (*above*), which now claims to be the live entertainment capital of the world. It boasts more than forty theaters. More than seven million people visit the town annually.

Major Airports

Airport	Location	Passengers per year (2000)
Lambert-St. Louis International	St. Louis	30,561,387
Kansas City International	Kansas City	12,350,725
Springfield-Branson Regional	Springfield	713,808

How Does Missouri Run?

> Bribery is treason, and the givers and
> takers of bribes are...traitors... If a party
> cannot get along without rascals, the people
> should get along without the party.
>
> — *Joseph Folk, Governor of Missouri, 1905–09*

The first Missouri Constitution was adopted in 1820, a little more than thirty years after the U.S. Constitution was ratified. Like that document, the Missouri Constitution established a government with three branches: executive, legislative, and judicial. Since that first constitution, Missourians have adopted three others — in 1865, 1875, and 1945. Under the most recent constitution, Missouri residents vote once every twenty years on whether to call a constitutional convention to amend the document. An amendment procedure may be initiated by a majority of the members of the state legislature, or General Assembly. Citizens may also submit amendments. In that case, a petition signed by 8 percent of the voters in two-thirds of the state's congressional districts brings an amendment to a vote. An amendment must be approved by a majority of voters to become part of the constitution.

Executive Branch

Missouri's governor serves a four-year term, like the president of the United States. Also like the president, the governor is limited to two terms. As part of the governor's duties, he or she names people to executive branch positions. The governor is the highest-ranking government official in Missouri.

Following the governor in importance are the lieutenant governor, secretary of state, attorney general, state treasurer, and state auditor. The lieutenant governor serves the citizens of the state in much the same way the U.S. vice president assists the president. The secretary of state

DID YOU KNOW?

Missouri has nine members in the U.S. House of Representatives and two senators. The state has eleven votes in the electoral college.

Elected Posts in the Executive Branch		
Office	Length of Term	Term Limits
Governor	4 years	2 terms
Lieutenant Governor	4 years	None
Secretary of State	4 years	None
Attorney General	4 years	None
State Treasurer	4 years	2 terms
State Auditor	4 years	None

collects, compiles, stores, and publishes legal and legislative documents for state residents. The secretary of state is also Missouri's chief elections official. Missouri's attorney general represents the state in state and federal courts. The attorney general's office is the state's law firm. The state treasurer is the state government's primary financial officer. The office of the treasurer manages the state's annual revenues, directs banking services, and manages the state's investment portfolio. The auditor keeps track of state revenue.

Legislative Branch

Missouri's state legislature is called the General Assembly. There are 34 senators and 163 representatives. Senators are elected to four-year terms and can serve no more than two terms. Representatives serve for two years, and they can serve no more than four terms. Total service in the legislature is limited to sixteen years.

Missouri's General Assembly meets for approximately five months every year, beginning in January and ending in May. The main responsibility of the General Assembly is to make laws and initiate constitutional

▼ The Missouri capitol building, in Jefferson City, was completed in 1917 and is made of limestone from Carthage. A statue of Thomas Jefferson stands on the front steps.

amendments. Bills become law if they are approved by a majority of the members of both houses and are signed by the governor. The General Assembly also balances the power of the other two branches of government by having some executive and judicial powers. For example, it approves the governor's appointments, and it can impeach the governor and state judges.

Judicial Branch

Seven judges sit on Missouri's supreme court, the state's highest court. The court of appeals is divided into three districts spread across the state. The governor of Missouri names judges for both the supreme court and the appellate courts. Judges serve twelve-year terms. Judges who complete one term must then be approved by Missouri voters to remain in office. Every two years, the justices on the supreme court designate one of their members to act as chief justice.

Missouri's Constitution also created local circuit courts, associate circuit courts, and municipal courts. Circuit court judges serve six-year terms, and the other judges serve four years. Chief judges of circuit and associate circuit courts in four counties and in the city of St. Louis are selected in the same way as supreme court judges. These judges are selected by the governor from a list made up by a commission of people from all political parties. All judges in other Missouri counties are elected.

County Government

Missouri has 114 counties and one independent city, St. Louis. County residents elect their local officials, including county commissioners, sheriffs, deeds recorders, revenue collectors, treasurers, coroners, prosecuting attorneys, surveyors, and public administrators. Missouri's constitution allows counties with more than eighty-five thousand residents to organize their own governments.

Election Tragedy

During the election of 2000, John Ashcroft ran for a second Senate term against the governor of the state, Mel Carnahan. Three weeks before election day, Carnahan and his son were killed in a plane crash. There was not enough time to name a replacement candidate, so Carnahan's name remained on the ballot. He won and the acting governor of the state named Carnahan's widow Jean *(above)*, who had never held public office, to the seat won by her late husband. President George W. Bush appointed Ashcroft as the U.S. attorney general.

General Assembly			
House	Number of Members	Length of Term	Term Limits
Senate	34 senators	4 years	2 terms
House of Representatives	163 representatives	2 years	4 terms

For Assembly members taking office after 1992, there is a lifetime limit of four terms in the House and two in the Senate.

The White House via Missouri

HARRY S. TRUMAN (1945–1953)

Few men have ever taken office under more intimidating circumstances than Harry Truman (1884–1972). He was in his second term as a U.S. senator from Missouri when President Franklin Roosevelt, seeking a fourth term in office, chose him as his running mate in 1944. Roosevelt won the election but died shortly after being sworn in. Truman had been vice president for only eighty-three days when he became the thirty-third president on April 12, 1945. During the first few weeks of his administration, World War II came to an end in Europe as the Allied forces defeated Nazi Germany. Truman then made the difficult decision to use the powerful new atomic bomb against Japan to end the war in the Pacific. The United States dropped atomic bombs on the Japanese cities of Hiroshima and Nagasaki, destroying the cities and bringing the war to an immediate end.

After the war, Truman established generous relief programs that helped rebuild countries crippled by the war, and forged military alliances to benefit national security. In one of the great electoral upsets in U.S. political history, he won election to a full term as president in 1948. That same year he issued an executive order to desegregate the military. He was two years into his second term when Communist forces from North Korea invaded South Korea in 1950. The president ordered U.S. troops to help South Korea. The Korean War lasted for three years, costing thirty-seven thousand U.S. lives.

Throughout his political career, Truman's strong, decisive style won him both friends and enemies. Today many historians rank the former Army major, haberdasher, judge, and senator from Missouri as one of the ten best U.S. presidents.

State Revenues

Missouri's general revenue, or state income, is obtained from several sources. Federal grants make up approximately one-third of the state's revenue. Much of the remaining income comes from a state sales tax and personal income tax. Missouri also taxes motor fuel, corporate income, motor vehicle licenses, and insurance. A popular state lottery also contributes a significant amount of money to the state's general revenue. In 2001 the lottery contributed $156.9 million to the state's department of education.

Much to See in the Show-Me State

> We camped in . . . one of the most beautiful places I ever saw in my life, open with hills & vallies all presenting themselves to the River.
>
> — *Explorer John Ordway on the banks of the Missouri River, 1804*

As Lewis and Clark's party learned, there is a great deal to do outdoors in Missouri. Today, however, there is plenty to do indoors as well. Missouri cities and towns offer popular entertainment, historical and educational sites, parks, musical venues, zoos, science centers, and museums. The largest art museums in Missouri are the St. Louis Art Museum and the Nelson-Atkins Museum of Art in Kansas City. The St. Louis Art Museum is home to artwork from many countries and time periods, while the Nelson-Atkins Museum focuses particularly on Chinese and American art. Missouri's capitol building in Jefferson City houses the State Museum, which displays historical, geological, and scientific exhibits. Other popular exhibits are on display at the Missouri Historical Society, located in Forest Park. The Harry S. Truman Library & Museum in Independence has information and exhibits about the former president. More than thirty thousand objects and papers from Truman's presidency are displayed there.

Branson, located in the state's southwest region, has more than forty theaters. Well-known musicians

▼ A giant badminton birdie (shuttlecock) outside the Nelson-Atkins Museum of Art in Kansas City amuses visitors.

regularly perform there. Lake of the Ozarks, located in central Missouri, is a large, artificially created lake. It is a popular resort and recreation destination. The state's lakes, rivers, and streams attract fishermen and sun-seekers from around the country.

Sports

Missouri is a great state for sports fans. Professional baseball and football are well represented by teams in St. Louis and Kansas City. Baseball's St. Louis Cardinals are one of the most popular teams in professional sports, with some of the most dedicated fans. The "Cards" have won the World Series nine times and boast many players who have been inducted into the National Baseball Hall of Fame. In 1998, the eyes of the baseball world were focused on St. Louis as first baseman Mark McGwire broke the thirty-seven-year-old record for most home runs in a season, hitting seventy. McGwire's record was broken by Barry Bonds in 2001. On the western side of the state, the Kansas City Royals are also popular with fans and have had several Hall of Fame players on the team. In 1985 Missouri was treated to a World Series between the Royals and the Cardinals, with the Royals taking the world title in seven games.

Pro football has also had a successful history in Missouri. The Kansas City Chiefs started out as the Dallas Texans and

▲ Mark McGwire of the St. Louis Cardinals, hitting his record-breaking sixty-second home run in 1998. He finished the season with a total of seventy home runs.

Sport	Team	Home
Baseball	St. Louis Cardinals	Busch Stadium, St. Louis
	Kansas City Royals	Kauffman Stadium, Kansas City
Football	St. Louis Rams	TransWorld Dome, St. Louis
	Kansas City Chiefs	Arrowhead Stadium, Kansas City
Hockey	St. Louis Blues	Savvis Center, St. Louis
Soccer	Kansas City Wizards	Arrowhead Stadium, Kansas City

were a charter team of the original American Football League (AFL) in 1960. They moved to Kansas City in 1963 and were renamed the Chiefs. After the merger of the AFL and the National Football League (NFL), the Chiefs became one of the sport's most successful and popular teams. The Chiefs won Super Bowl IV in 1970.

On the other side of the state, the St. Louis Rams, who moved to the city from Los Angeles in 1995, have become one of pro football's most exciting teams, winning Super Bowl XXXIV in 2000. They lost to the New England Patriots in 2002, in their second Super Bowl appearance as the St. Louis Rams.

▲ The St. Louis Rams defeated the Tennessee Titans to win Super Bowl XXXIV in 2000.

For those who prefer knocking down pins to knocking baseballs or knocking heads, St. Louis is also home to the International Bowling Museum and Hall of Fame. The three-story, 50,000-square-foot (4,645-square-meter) structure — located across from the Cardinals' home field, Busch Stadium — has exhibits on the five thousand-year history of bowling, information about famous bowlers, and four working bowling lanes.

Parks and Attractions

Missouri has forty-nine state parks and thirty-three historic sites. Mark Twain National Forest covers several locations in the central and southern areas of the state. The Ulysses S. Grant National Historic Site, a log cabin that was Grant's home prior to the Civil War, is located near St. Louis. Another important landmark is George Washington Carver National Monument, located near Diamond. The monument was erected to honor the famous Missouri-born, African-American scientist.

The Winston Churchill Memorial Library is located in Fulton. This structure, formerly the Church of St. Mary Aldermanbury in London, England, was taken apart piece by piece and moved to Missouri from London. It was rebuilt on the campus of Westminster College between 1964 and 1969.

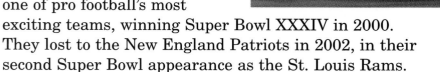

DID YOU KNOW?
The Gateway Arch in St. Louis is the fourth most visited tourist attraction in the world.

In 1946, Churchill, the former British prime minister, gave a speech on the campus in which he referred to an "iron curtain" that had descended across the continent of Europe. That term was used to describe the border between Eastern and Western Europe before the Soviet Union's collapse in 1991.

The Nation's Gateway

Stretched along the banks of the Mississippi River in St. Louis is the Jefferson National Expansion Memorial, which is home to one of the most famous landmarks in modern America — the Gateway Arch. The park itself opened on December 21, 1935. Construction of the Gateway Arch began on February 12, 1963 and was completed on October 28, 1965, when the structure's last piece was put into place. The base of the Gateway Arch is 630 feet (192 m) wide, the same as its height, and weighs a whopping 43,000 tons. At the time it was built, the Gateway Arch cost $13 million. The massive arch was built as a monument to America's westward expansion and exploration. In a 150-mile (241-km) per hour wind, the arch sways a maximum of 9 inches (23 cm) in each direction. On an average day, however, the structure moves only about half an inch (1.27 cm). Each year more than one million people journey to the top of the Gateway Arch. Trams were installed more than thirty years ago to carry people up the massive structure.

Beneath the arch on the riverfront is Levee Mercantile, an 1870s-style general store. Levee Mercantile offers visitors a step back in time. Many of the food products offered for

Under the Arch

Dwarfed by St. Louis's Gateway Arch is one of the world's most honored churches. The Old Cathedral, shown below, sits on a small piece of land near the southern end of the arch. Officially named the Basilica of Saint Louis, King of France, the church was built in 1770. The original structure was made of logs. Pope John XXIII made the Old Cathedral a basilica in 1961, which means it has special status within the Roman Catholic Church.

sale there are made using traditional nineteenth-century recipes and old-fashioned equipment. Candy is cooked in big iron kettles, and breads are baked in brick ovens.

Fun Underground and Outdoors

Missouri has more than five thousand caves, nineteen of which have guided tours. Time and natural processes have created stalactites and stalagmites, as well as other formations called soda straws, popcorn, and flowstone. Many of these caves are part of Missouri lore, such as the cave in Mark Twain's *Tom Sawyer,* the cave hideout of outlaw Jesse James, and the cave that holds the record for the most underground weddings.

Missouri offers a variety of seasonal activities and events. The premier attraction is Fair St. Louis, which takes place each year in July. This festival, known as "America's biggest birthday party," features concerts, foods, an air show, and fireworks. Other annual events include the Dogwood Festival, held in Camdenton, the Scott Joplin Ragtime Festival in Sedalia, National Tom Sawyer Days in Hannibal, the Bluegrass Festival at Sam A. Baker State Park in Patterson, and Maifest Celebration, in Hermann, which celebrates the area's German heritage.

▼ Fantastic Caverns is actually a single cave. Located near Springfield, it is the only cave in the United States that cars can drive through. The cave was carved out by an ancient underground river.

The Capital City

With all the attention given to St. Louis, Kansas City, and the Ozarks, it might be easy to overlook Jefferson City, the capital of Missouri. That would be a mistake. This city of about forty thousand people lies near the center of the state, along the Missouri River. It has been the capital since 1826, when it also became a station for stagecoaches and a steamboat landing for westward travelers. The state capitol is the most prominent building in the downtown area. Built of white limestone, it was modeled after the U.S. Capitol. Murals by Missouri artist Thomas Hart Benton portraying the state's history cover the walls of the third floor. Near the capitol are the governor's mansion and gardens, as well as the Harry S. Truman State Office Building.

▲ The beautiful Lake of the Ozarks is the northern gateway to the Ozark Plateau.

The capital region is a treasure for those who enjoy the outdoors. Jefferson City is located about 50 miles (80 km) northeast of the Lake of the Ozarks. This huge, artificially created lake offers boating, fishing, waterskiing, and swimming. There are thousands of quiet coves along its 1,375 miles (2,212 km) of beautiful shoreline.

One of the most popular outdoor attractions in the Jefferson City area is the Katy Trail State Park. The trail is built on the former line of the Missouri-Kansas-Texas (MKT — or "Katy") Railroad. When the railroad ceased operation in 1986, it presented an opportunity to create a long-distance hiking and bicycling trail. Today the park runs 225 miles (362 km) from St. Charles to Clinton. The trail, winding through some of the most scenic areas of the state, runs beside the Missouri River. While the scenery changes, the trail remains level as it wanders through the Missouri countryside.

▶ The Missouri-Kansas-Texas Railroad once ran through Missouri; its trackbed is now the Katy hiking trail.

Show Stoppers

> I am no book larnt man, but there is few who can beat me swapping horses or guessing at the weight of a bar [bear].
> — *Jacob Groom, Missouri state legislator of the 1820s*

Following are only a few of the thousands of people who were born, died, or spent much of their lives in Missouri and made extraordinary contributions to the state and the nation.

MARK TWAIN
AUTHOR

BORN: *November 3, 1835, Florida*
DIED: *April 21, 1910, Redding, CT*

Born Samuel Langhorne Clemens, the writer Mark Twain grew up in Hannibal, watching riverboats on the Mississippi. Clemens's first job was as a printer's apprentice. Later he worked at his brother's newspaper. In 1857 he became a riverboat pilot on the Mississippi and went on to hold other jobs as a reporter, miner, and writer. He took his pen name, "Mark Twain," from the riverboat expression meaning "two fathoms." Twain was famous for his humorous tales and witty articles.

He wrote beloved novels such as *The Adventures of Tom Sawyer* and *The Adventures of Huckleberry Finn*, the latter considered by many to be one of the greatest U.S. novels ever written.

GEORGE WASHINGTON CARVER
EDUCATOR AND AGRICULTURAL CHEMIST

BORN: *circa 1865, Diamond Grove*
DIED: *January 5, 1943, Tuskegee, AL*

George Washington Carver, son of a slave, was orphaned by the time he was five. He lived with his mother's former master, Moses Carver, until he was ten or twelve, when he left to seek an education. Carver read many books and worked many jobs, educating himself until his late twenties, when he earned a high school diploma.

Carver attended Simpson College and Iowa Agricultural College, graduating from the latter in 1894. He earned a Master of Science degree in 1896. Later he became director of the Department of Agriculture at Tuskegee Institute, an African-American college in Alabama. Carver became known for his research on soil management. He encouraged farmers to grow legumes such as peanuts and soybeans because they actually replenish the soil as they grow. Carver also helped develop markets for these crops.

T. S. ELIOT
POET

BORN: *September 26, 1888, St. Louis*
DIED: *January 4, 1965, London, England*

Thomas Stearns Eliot lived in St. Louis for the first eighteen years of his life. In 1910, after receiving degrees from Harvard University, Eliot left the United States. He spent a year in Paris, returned to Harvard, and then moved permanently to Europe. Eliot first worked as a teacher and later for Lloyd's Bank, all the while writing poetry and criticism. Two of his poems, "The Love Song of J. Alfred Prufrock" (1917) and "The Waste Land" (1922), are considered to be among the greatest poems ever written in English. His *Old Possum's Book of Practical Cats* is also a favorite — the long-running Broadway musical *Cats* was based on it. Eliot became a British subject in 1927 and was awarded the Nobel Prize for Literature in 1948.

THOMAS HART BENTON
PAINTER

BORN: *April 15, 1889, Neosho*
DIED: *January 19, 1975, Kansas City*

Thomas Hart Benton's father was a congressman, and his great-uncle, for whom he was named, had been a famous U.S. senator. Benton, however, decided at an early age to become an artist rather than a politician. He worked as a cartoonist for the Joplin, Missouri *American* and then attended classes at the Art Institute of Chicago in 1906 and 1907. At age nineteen, Benton went to Paris, where he studied art. When he returned to the United States, he became involved with modern artists and also painted sets for movies. Benton traveled through the South and Midwest and became famous as a muralist and as a leading artist in the American Regionalist movement. Regionalists such as Benton painted American life in a semi-realistic and heroic manner. Benton painted the *Missouri Mural* in the state capitol in Jefferson City.

ROY WILKINS
CIVIL RIGHTS LEADER

BORN: *August 30, 1901, St. Louis*
DIED: *September 8, 1981, New York, NY*

Roy Wilkins was raised by his aunt and uncle in St. Paul, Minnesota. He attended integrated schools in that city and majored in sociology at the University of Minnesota. He worked as an editor at the student newspaper there and also on the *St. Paul Appeal*, a local African-American newspaper. After graduation he became a reporter and editor of the *Kansas City Call* in

Missouri. In 1931, while living in Missouri, he joined the National Association for the Advancement of Colored People (NAACP). He became executive director of the organization in 1955. One of the greatest moments of his career was the 1963 civil rights march on Washington, D.C. that he helped organize.

WALT DISNEY
IMAGINEER

BORN: *December 5, 1901, Chicago, IL*
DIED: *December 15, 1966, Los Angeles, CA*

Walter Elias Disney was born in Chicago, Illinois, but was raised on a farm in Marceline, Missouri, and in Kansas City. In Kansas City, he studied art from mail order courses and in classes at a museum. His first cartoon featured a mouse named Mickey piloting a steamboat like the ones Disney had observed in his youth. After serving overseas in World War I as a Red Cross ambulance driver, Disney returned to Kansas City in 1919 to work for a commercial illustrator. Around this time, he began to create and market his first animated works. By 1922, he had set up his own shop in association with Ub Iwerks, whose drawing ability and technical inventiveness were prime factors in Disney's eventual success. In 1955, Disney opened Disneyland in Anaheim, California, the first theme park of its kind. It proved to be the most successful amusement park in history, with 6.7 million visitors by 1966, the year of his death.

JOSEPHINE BAKER
SINGER AND DANCER

BORN: *June 3, 1906, St. Louis*
DIED: *April 12, 1975, Paris, France*

This famous African-American singer and dancer was born Freda Josephine McDonald in St. Louis. At the age of thirteen, she began her professional career performing on Broadway in such shows as *Shuffle Along* and *Chocolate Dandies*. In the 1920s, Baker moved to Paris to escape racism. She became one of the most popular nightclub entertainers in France. During World War II, Baker worked with the French Red Cross and as an intelligence agent, once carrying military reports, written in invisible ink on her sheet music, from France to Portugal. She was awarded the *Croix de Guerre* by the French government. More than twenty thousand people attended her funeral service in Paris, which was broadcast on French television.

YOGI BERRA
BASEBALL PLAYER

BORN: *May 12, 1925, St. Louis*

Lawrence Peter Berra's childhood friend, Bobby Hofman, gave him the nickname that would stick for life. Berra began his career in 1942, playing minor league baseball. His talent caught the eye of baseball scouts. Asked to play for his hometown team, the St. Louis Cardinals, he decided instead to accept an offer from the New York Yankees. At eighteen, Berra enlisted in the U. S. Navy, and in June 1944 he participated in the

D-Day landing at Omaha Beach in France. Yogi returned to baseball after the war, joining the Yankees as a catcher. Over the course of his career, Berra was a fifteen-time All Star and played in fourteen World Series, setting many records. Berra was elected to the National Baseball Hall of Fame in 1972. In addition to these legendary sports achievements, Berra is famous for his malapropisms, expressions such as "Baseball is 90 percent mental; the other half is physical."

Chuck Berry
MUSICIAN

BORN: *October 18, 1926, St. Louis*

Charles Edward Anderson Berry, known as Chuck, grew up on the north side of St. Louis. As a child, Berry sang in his church choir and studied music in high school. He also listened to both blues and country music on the radio. As a teenager, Berry served several years in jail for armed robbery. After his release, he returned to St. Louis to work and to play music in local clubs. He moved to Chicago, where he met legendary bluesman Muddy Waters. Waters got Berry a recording contract, and in 1955 he recorded his first song, "Maybellene." The song was an instant hit. Berry went on to record many other hits, including "Roll Over Beethoven" and

"Johnny B. Goode." His mixture of country-western and blues styles, clever lyrics, and great showmanship inspired countless musicians worldwide. He was inducted into the Rock and Roll Hall of Fame in 1986.

Maya Angelou
POET

BORN: *April 4, 1928, St. Louis*

Born Marguerite Johnson, Maya Angelou grew up in St. Louis and Stamps, Arkansas. When she was twelve, she moved to San Francisco with her mother. She changed her name when she started to work as a dancer. In the 1950s, Angelou visited New York and became involved with a group of writers who were committed to representing the African-American experience in literature. Angelou also joined the touring company of the opera *Porgy and Bess* and traveled throughout Europe and Africa. In 1970, she published a novel, *I Know Why the Caged Bird Sings,* which was based on traumatic experiences in her childhood. In 1992, she was invited to compose and read a poem at the presidential inauguration of Bill Clinton. She recited her poem "On the Pulse of Morning" to worldwide acclaim. Angelou is a professor at Wake Forest University in North Carolina.

Missouri

History At-A-Glance

1673
Father Jacques Marquette and Louis Jolliet are the first Europeans to explore the mouth of the Missouri River.

1682
René-Robert Cavelier, Sieur de La Salle, claims the region for France, naming it Louisiana.

1735
Missouri's first permanent white settlement is established at Ste. Genevieve.

1762
France cedes the Louisiana region to Spain.

1764
Pierre Laclede Liguest and René Auguste Chouteau settle the city of St. Louis.

1803
France sells the Missouri region to the United States as part of the Louisiana Purchase.

1804
The Lewis and Clark expedition departs from St. Louis.

1811
The first of several large earthquakes shakes Missouri, and beyond.

1812
Congress declares the Missouri region a U.S. territory.

1821
On August 10 Missouri enters the Union as the 24th state.

1851
The first U.S. traveler's aid society is started in St. Louis.

1854
Fighting begins between antislavery Kansas residents and pro-slavery Missourians.

1600	1700	1800

1492
Christopher Columbus comes to New World.

1607
Capt. John Smith and three ships land on Virginia coast and start first English settlement in New World — Jamestown.

1754–63
French and Indian War.

1773
Boston Tea Party.

1776
Declaration of Independence adopted July 4.

1777
Articles of Confederation adopted by Continental Congress.

1787
U.S. Constitution written.

1812–14
War of 1812.

United States

History At-A-Glance

1861–1865
More than one thousand Civil War battles — 11 percent of all battles in the war — are fought in Missouri.

1865
Missouri Republicans write a new constitution that abolishes slavery.

1882
Outlaw Jesse James is killed by Robert Ford, a member of his gang, in St. Joseph.

1904
Louisiana Purchase Exposition, also known as the World's Fair, is held in St. Louis.

1931
Bagnell Dam on the Osage River is completed. The dam forms the Lake of the Ozarks.

1945
Vice President Harry S. Truman, a Missouri native, becomes the 33rd U.S. president on the death of President Franklin D. Roosevelt.

1945
Missouri adopts the constitution it has today.

1948
Truman wins one of the closest elections in history to a full term as U.S. president.

1965
St.Louis's Gateway Arch is completed. At 630 feet (192 m) high, it is the nation's tallest monument.

1983
The Environmental Protection Agency buys and evacuates the town of Times Beach because of dioxin contamination.

1986
Missouri begins a statewide lottery.

2000
Mel Carnahan is elected U.S. senator from Missouri after his death in a plane crash.

1800   **1900**   **2000**

1848
Gold discovered in California draws eighty thousand prospectors in the 1849 Gold Rush.

1861–65
Civil War.

1869
Transcontinental railroad completed.

1917–18
U.S. involvement in World War I.

1929
Stock market crash ushers in Great Depression.

1941–45
U.S. involvement in World War II.

1950–53
U.S. fights in the Korean War.

1964–73
U.S. involvement in Vietnam War.

2000
George W. Bush wins the closest presidential election in history.

2001
A terrorist attack in which four hijacked airliners crash into New York City's World Trade Center, the Pentagon, and farmland in western Pennsylvania leaves thousands dead or injured.

▼ The American Legion parade in Kansas City in 1921 celebrated the Allied victory in World War I.

Festivals and Fun for All

Check web site for exact date and directions.

Cotton Carnival, Sikeston
The town of Sikeston is the northernmost place in the United States where cotton is grown for market. The town celebrates its unique status with an annual carnival, featuring one of the state's longest parades.
www.sikestonmo.net/calendar.html

Country Club Plaza Art Fair, Kansas City
Art lovers crowd streets filled with artwork in this annual festival, which draws more than twelve hundred artists.
www.countryclubplaza.com/artfair.html

American Royal Livestock, Horse Show, and Rodeo, Kansas City
This annual event features a rodeo, a horse show, concerts, a livestock show, a parade, and a barbecue.
www.americanroyal.com

Bluegrass Festival at Sam A. Baker State Park, Patterson
The Missouri Area Bluegrass Committee hosts this celebration of bluegrass music, which includes performances by local artists as well as a fiddling competition.
www.bluegrassamerica.com

Cabin Fever Quilt Show, Independence
Warm up in the winter by attending this exhibition of local handmade quilts.
www.americanjourneys.com/MO-Kansas-City/events.html

Dogwood Festival, Camdenton
Locals invite the world to come celebrate with them each spring as local dogwoods burst into bloom.
www.camdentonchamber.com/Dogwood.htm

Festival of American Music and Craftsmanship, Branson
Each year Silver Dollar City hosts a festival that showcases folk music and crafts such as barrel making, leatherwork, and jewelry.
www.silverdollarcity.com/festivals/musiccraft.asp

▶ Getting into the spirit of Hannibal's Tom Sawyer Days.

The Great Forest Park Balloon Race, St. Louis

Every year crowds gather to see this balloon race and the St. Louis Symphony, which plays a send-off concert for the racers.
www.forestparkforever.org/intro.html

Jour de Fete, Ste. Genevieve

Ste. Genevieve celebrates community with an arts and crafts show, classic car show, and fun run.
rosecity.net/rhr/events/jour_de_fete

Maifest Celebration, Hermann

The town of Hermann celebrates its German heritage with this May festival of music, food, and dancing.
www.missourimeramecregion.org/cities/hermann.html

Missouri State Fair, Sedalia

The Missouri State Fair has been celebrating Missouri agriculture and entertainment for one hundred years.
www.mostatefair.com

National Tom Sawyer Days, Hannibal

This festival, celebrating Mark Twain's beloved character, one of the best-loved boys in U.S. fiction, includes a fence-painting contest, a frog-jumping contest, and a Tomboy Sawyer competition.
www.VisitHannibal.com/events.html

Riverfest, Cape Girardeau

Cape Girardeau, a town of many murals, celebrates itself with a festival of music and food every year in June.
www.cityof
capegirardeau.org

Scott Joplin Ragtime Festival, Sedalia

Sedalia honors its famous former resident with a four-day festival of his music in June. Outdoor concerts, tea dances, and sheet-music swaps are all part of the fun.
www.scottjoplin.org

Storytelling Festival, St. Louis

The nation's premier storytellers come to town for this event, sponsored by the University of Missouri at St. Louis.
www.umsl.edu/~conted/storyfes

Valley of Flowers Festival, Florissant

Florissant welcomes the spring with this local festival, which features flower-covered floats in a joyous parade.
www.florissantmo.com/thingsToDo/events/valley%20of%20Flowers/valleyOfFlowers.htm

Books

January, Brendan. *The Dred Scott Decision*. New York: Children's Press, 1998. This book tells the fascinating story of the life of Dred Scott and the court decision that played a part in the national crisis over slavery.

Nicholson, Lois. *George Washington Carver*. Broomall, PA: Chelsea House Publishers, 1993. George Washington Carver was a scientist who changed the way people thought about farming. The story of his life and work is told here in an illustrated biography.

Ross, Stewart. *Mark Twain and Huckleberry Finn*. New York: Viking Children's Books, 1999. Discover how Mark Twain used his childhood experiences in Missouri to create the classic character of Huckleberry Finn.

Sandweiss, Lee Ann. *St. Louis Architecture for Kids*. St. Louis: Missouri Historical Society, 2001. The Gateway Arch is just one of the many interesting buildings in St. Louis. This book takes readers on an informative tour of the city.

Wilder, Laura Ingalls and Rose Wilder Lane. *On the Way Home: The Diary of a Trip from South Dakota to Mansfield, Missouri, in 1894*. New York: Harper Trophy, 1994. Laura Ingalls Wilder was the author of the famous *Little House on the Prairie* books. In her diaries readers can discover more about her life and the realities on which she based her fiction.

Web Sites

▶ Official state web site
www.state.mo.us

▶ Jefferson City official web site
www.jeffcitymo.org

▶ Missouri Historical Society
www.mohistory.org

INDEX

Note: Page numbers in *italics* refer to maps, illustrations, or photographs.